SWIMMING LOGBOOK

NAME:

START DATE:

©poweredbychlorine.com

Powered By Chlorine
Swimming Logbook
By AlyT & Born To Swim

Written by AlyT
Copyright 2024 by Allison Tyson. All rights reserved.

First printing: April, 2024

Disclaimer
While we draw on our professional expertise and background in teaching learn to swim and swimming training, by purchasing and reading our products you acknowledge that we have produced this book for informational and educational purposes only. You alone are solely responsible and take full responsibility for your own wellbeing as well as the health, lives and well-being of your family and children in your care in and around water.

Stay in touch:
Born to Swim, P.O Box 6699, Cairns City, QLD 4870
SwimMechanics@yahoo.com
www.BornToSwim.com.au
www.PoweredByChlorine.com
Instagram @LearnToSwimTheAustralianWay
Etsy Store www.borntoswimglobal.etsy.com
Most titles available from Etsy, Amazon and all good online Book Retailers

Other titles by this Author:
Water Awareness Newborns
Water Awareness Babies
Water Awareness Toddlers
Learn to Swim the Australian Way Level 1 The Foundations
Learn to Swim the Australian Way Level 2 The Basics
Learn to Swim the Australian Way Level 3 Intermediate
Learn to Swim the Australian Way Level 4 Advanced
The Ultimate Pool Party Planner
Focus On Freestyle: Teaching Guide
Water Safety: Teaching Guide
Breaststroke Bootcamp: Teaching Guide
Butterfly Bootcamp: Teaching Guide
Backstroke Bootcamp: Teaching Guide
Learning To Float: Color Me In & Learn To Swim Activity Book
A Float For Every Stroke: Teaching Body Position
Visual Aids For Inclusive Aquatic Education: 100+ Swimming Flashcards
Welcome To Swim Squad: Activity Book For Swimmers
Eat Pray Swim: A Swimmer's Logbook & Prayer Journal
Thalassophile: Logbook & Journal For Lovers Of The Ocean and Sea
Wild Swimming Quotes Coloring Book For Adults : Activity Book For Open Water Swimmers
Powered By Chlorine : Logbooks & Journals For Swimmers

TRAINING DAYS TRACKER

Month

S	M	T	W	Th	F	S

Month

S	M	T	W	Th	F	S

Month

S	M	T	W	Th	F	S

Month

S	M	T	W	Th	F	S

Month

S	M	T	W	Th	F	S

Month

S	M	T	W	Th	F	S

©poweredbychlorine.com

TRAINING DAYS TRACKER

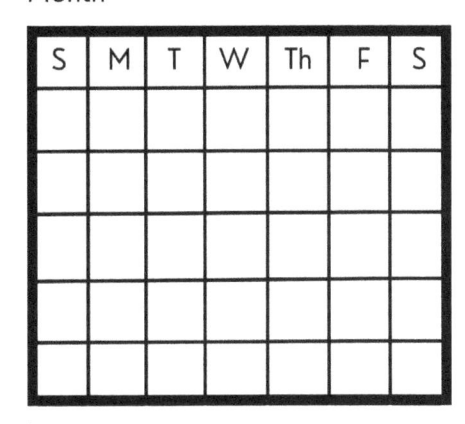

Month

S	M	T	W	Th	F	S

Month

S	M	T	W	Th	F	S

Month

S	M	T	W	Th	F	S

Month

S	M	T	W	Th	F	S

Month

S	M	T	W	Th	F	S

Month

S	M	T	W	Th	F	S

©poweredbychlorine.com

MONTHLY GOAL SETTING

Goal	Goal
Actionable Steps	Actionable Steps

Goal	Goal
Actionable Steps	Actionable Steps

Goal	Goal
Actionable Steps	Actionable Steps

©poweredbychlorine.com

MONTHLY GOAL SETTING

Goal

Actionable Steps

Goal

Actionable Steps

Goal

Actionable Steps

Goal

Actionable Steps

Goal

Actionable Steps

Goal

Actionable Steps

© poweredbychlorine.com

YEAR AT A GLANCE

Month ....

Month ....

Month ....

Month ....

Month ....

Month ....

YEAR AT A GLANCE

Month ....

Month ....

Month ....

Month ....

Month ....

Month.....................

©poweredbychlorine.com

DAILY SWIM TRAINING LOG

Date: Location: Today's Focus:

Time: Pool: 50   25   other   Coach:

Mood: Day: M   Tu   W   Th   Fr   Sa   Su

Warm Up

REPS	DISTANCE STROKE/DRILL/KICK	INTERVAL	INTENSITY	NOTES/FEEDBACK

Pre Set

REPS	DISTANCE STROKE/DRILL/KICK	INTERVAL	INTENSITY	NOTES/FEEDBACK

Main Set

REPS	DISTANCE STROKE/DRILL/KICK	INTERVAL	INTENSITY	NOTES/FEEDBACK

Cool Down

Total Distance: Total Laps:

©poweredbychlorine.com

Dryland Training

REPS	EXERCISES	WEIGHTS/TIME	INTENSITY	NOTES/FEEDBACK

Nutrition Tracker

Breakfast	Dinner
Lunch	Snacks & Drinks

Training Schedule

TYPE	AM TIME	PM TIME	LOCATION

DAILY SWIM TRAINING LOG

Date:　　　　　Location:　　　　　Today's Focus:

Time:　　　　　Pool: 50　25　other　　Coach:

Mood:　　　　　　　　　　　　　　　Day:　M　Tu　W　Th　Fr　Sa　Su

Warm Up

REPS	DISTANCE STROKE/DRILL/KICK	INTERVAL	INTENSITY	NOTES/FEEDBACK

Pre Set

REPS	DISTANCE STROKE/DRILL/KICK	INTERVAL	INTENSITY	NOTES/FEEDBACK

Main Set

REPS	DISTANCE STROKE/DRILL/KICK	INTERVAL	INTENSITY	NOTES/FEEDBACK

Cool Down

Total Distance:　　　　　　　　　　　　　　Total Laps:

©poweredbychlorine.com

Dryland Training

REPS	EXERCISES	WEIGHTS/TIME	INTENSITY	NOTES/FEEDBACK

Nutrition Tracker

Breakfast	Dinner
Lunch	Snacks & Drinks

Training Schedule

TYPE	AM TIME	PM TIME	LOCATION

DAILY SWIM TRAINING LOG

Date: Location: Today's Focus:

Time: Pool: 50   25   other   Coach:

Mood: Day: M   Tu   W   Th   Fr   Sa   Su

Warm Up

REPS	DISTANCE STROKE/DRILL/KICK	INTERVAL	INTENSITY	NOTES/FEEDBACK

Pre Set

REPS	DISTANCE STROKE/DRILL/KICK	INTERVAL	INTENSITY	NOTES/FEEDBACK

Main Set

REPS	DISTANCE STROKE/DRILL/KICK	INTERVAL	INTENSITY	NOTES/FEEDBACK

Cool Down

Total Distance: Total Laps:

Dryland Training

REPS	EXERCISES	WEIGHTS/TIME	INTENSITY	NOTES/FEEDBACK

Nutrition Tracker

Breakfast	Dinner
Lunch	Snacks & Drinks

Training Schedule

TYPE	AM TIME	PM TIME	LOCATION

©poweredbychlorine.com

DAILY SWIM TRAINING LOG

Date: Location: Today's Focus:

Time: Pool: 50   25   other   Coach:

Mood: Day: M   Tu   W   Th   Fr   Sa   Su

Warm Up

REPS	DISTANCE STROKE/DRILL/KICK	INTERVAL	INTENSITY	NOTES/FEEDBACK

Pre Set

REPS	DISTANCE STROKE/DRILL/KICK	INTERVAL	INTENSITY	NOTES/FEEDBACK

Main Set

REPS	DISTANCE STROKE/DRILL/KICK	INTERVAL	INTENSITY	NOTES/FEEDBACK

Cool Down

Total Distance: Total Laps:

©poweredbychlorine.com

Dryland Training

REPS	EXERCISES	WEIGHTS/TIME	INTENSITY	NOTES/FEEDBACK

Nutrition Tracker

Breakfast	Dinner
Lunch	Snacks & Drinks

Training Schedule

TYPE	AM TIME	PM TIME	LOCATION

©poweredbychlorine.com

DAILY SWIM TRAINING LOG

Date: Location: Today's Focus:

Time: Pool: 50   25   other Coach:

Mood: Day: M   Tu   W   Th   Fr   Sa   Su

Warm Up

REPS	DISTANCE STROKE/DRILL/KICK	INTERVAL	INTENSITY	NOTES/FEEDBACK

Pre Set

REPS	DISTANCE STROKE/DRILL/KICK	INTERVAL	INTENSITY	NOTES/FEEDBACK

Main Set

REPS	DISTANCE STROKE/DRILL/KICK	INTERVAL	INTENSITY	NOTES/FEEDBACK

Cool Down

Total Distance: Total Laps:

© poweredbychlorine.com

Dryland Training

REPS	EXERCISES	WEIGHTS/TIME	INTENSITY	NOTES/FEEDBACK

Nutrition Tracker

Breakfast	Dinner
Lunch	Snacks & Drinks

Training Schedule

TYPE	AM TIME	PM TIME	LOCATION

DAILY SWIM TRAINING LOG

Date: Location: Today's Focus:

Time: Pool: 50   25   other   Coach:

Mood: Day: M   Tu   W   Th   Fr   Sa   Su

Warm Up

REPS	DISTANCE STROKE/DRILL/KICK	INTERVAL	INTENSITY	NOTES/FEEDBACK

Pre Set

REPS	DISTANCE STROKE/DRILL/KICK	INTERVAL	INTENSITY	NOTES/FEEDBACK

Main Set

REPS	DISTANCE STROKE/DRILL/KICK	INTERVAL	INTENSITY	NOTES/FEEDBACK

Cool Down

Total Distance: Total Laps:

©poweredbychlorine.com

Dryland Training

REPS	EXERCISES	WEIGHTS/TIME	INTENSITY	NOTES/FEEDBACK

Nutrition Tracker

Breakfast	Dinner
Lunch	Snacks & Drinks

Training Schedule

TYPE	AM TIME	PM TIME	LOCATION

DAILY SWIM TRAINING LOG

Date: Location: Today's Focus:

Time: Pool: 50   25   other   Coach:

Mood: 😊 😊 😊 😊 😊   Day: M Tu W Th Fr Sa Su

Warm Up

REPS	DISTANCE STROKE/DRILL/KICK	INTERVAL	INTENSITY	NOTES/FEEDBACK

Pre Set

REPS	DISTANCE STROKE/DRILL/KICK	INTERVAL	INTENSITY	NOTES/FEEDBACK

Main Set

REPS	DISTANCE STROKE/DRILL/KICK	INTERVAL	INTENSITY	NOTES/FEEDBACK

Cool Down

Total Distance: Total Laps:

© poweredbychlorine.com

Dryland Training

REPS	EXERCISES	WEIGHTS/TIME	INTENSITY	NOTES/FEEDBACK

Nutrition Tracker

Breakfast	Dinner
Lunch	Snacks & Drinks

Training Schedule

TYPE	AM TIME	PM TIME	LOCATION

© poweredbychlorine.com

DAILY SWIM TRAINING LOG

Date: Location: Today's Focus:

Time: Pool: 50 25 other Coach:

Mood: Day: M Tu W Th Fr Sa Su

Warm Up

REPS	DISTANCE STROKE/DRILL/KICK	INTERVAL	INTENSITY	NOTES/FEEDBACK

Pre Set

REPS	DISTANCE STROKE/DRILL/KICK	INTERVAL	INTENSITY	NOTES/FEEDBACK

Main Set

REPS	DISTANCE STROKE/DRILL/KICK	INTERVAL	INTENSITY	NOTES/FEEDBACK

Cool Down

Total Distance: Total Laps:

©poweredbychlorine.com

Dryland Training

REPS	EXERCISES	WEIGHTS/TIME	INTENSITY	NOTES/FEEDBACK

Nutrition Tracker

Breakfast	Dinner
Lunch	Snacks & Drinks

Training Schedule

TYPE	AM TIME	PM TIME	LOCATION

©poweredbychlorine.com

DAILY SWIM TRAINING LOG

Date:　　　　　Location:　　　　　Today's Focus:

Time:　　　　　Pool: 50　25　other　　Coach:

Mood:　　　　　　　　　　　　　　　Day:　M　Tu　W　Th　Fr　Sa　Su

Warm Up

REPS	DISTANCE STROKE/DRILL/KICK	INTERVAL	INTENSITY	NOTES/FEEDBACK

Pre Set

REPS	DISTANCE STROKE/DRILL/KICK	INTERVAL	INTENSITY	NOTES/FEEDBACK

Main Set

REPS	DISTANCE STROKE/DRILL/KICK	INTERVAL	INTENSITY	NOTES/FEEDBACK

Cool Down

Total Distance:　　　　　　　　　　Total Laps:

Dryland Training

REPS	EXERCISES	WEIGHTS/TIME	INTENSITY	NOTES/FEEDBACK

Nutrition Tracker

Breakfast	Dinner
Lunch	Snacks & Drinks

Training Schedule

TYPE	AM TIME	PM TIME	LOCATION

DAILY SWIM TRAINING LOG

Date: Location: Today's Focus:

Time: Pool: 50   25   other   Coach:

Mood: Day: M   Tu   W   Th   Fr   Sa   Su

Warm Up

REPS	DISTANCE STROKE/DRILL/KICK	INTERVAL	INTENSITY	NOTES/FEEDBACK

Pre Set

REPS	DISTANCE STROKE/DRILL/KICK	INTERVAL	INTENSITY	NOTES/FEEDBACK

Main Set

REPS	DISTANCE STROKE/DRILL/KICK	INTERVAL	INTENSITY	NOTES/FEEDBACK

Cool Down

Total Distance: Total Laps:

© poweredbychlorine.com

Dryland Training

REPS	EXERCISES	WEIGHTS/TIME	INTENSITY	NOTES/FEEDBACK

Nutrition Tracker

Breakfast	Dinner
Lunch	Snacks & Drinks

Training Schedule

TYPE	AM TIME	PM TIME	LOCATION

DAILY SWIM TRAINING LOG

Date:　　　　Location:　　　　　　Today's Focus:

Time:　　　　Pool: 50　25　other　Coach:

Mood:　　　　　　　　　　　　　Day:　M　Tu　W　Th　Fr　Sa　Su

Warm Up

REPS	DISTANCE STROKE/DRILL/KICK	INTERVAL	INTENSITY	NOTES/FEEDBACK

Pre Set

REPS	DISTANCE STROKE/DRILL/KICK	INTERVAL	INTENSITY	NOTES/FEEDBACK

Main Set

REPS	DISTANCE STROKE/DRILL/KICK	INTERVAL	INTENSITY	NOTES/FEEDBACK

Cool Down

Total Distance:　　　　　　　　　　　　　Total Laps:

Dryland Training

REPS	EXERCISES	WEIGHTS/TIME	INTENSITY	NOTES/FEEDBACK

Nutrition Tracker

Breakfast	Dinner
Lunch	Snacks & Drinks

Training Schedule

TYPE	AM TIME	PM TIME	LOCATION

DAILY SWIM TRAINING LOG

Date: Location: Today's Focus:

Time: Pool: 50   25   other   Coach:

Mood: Day: M   Tu   W   Th   Fr   Sa   Su

Warm Up

REPS	DISTANCE STROKE/DRILL/KICK	INTERVAL	INTENSITY	NOTES/FEEDBACK

Pre Set

REPS	DISTANCE STROKE/DRILL/KICK	INTERVAL	INTENSITY	NOTES/FEEDBACK

Main Set

REPS	DISTANCE STROKE/DRILL/KICK	INTERVAL	INTENSITY	NOTES/FEEDBACK

Cool Down

Total Distance: Total Laps:

©poweredbychlorine.com

Dryland Training

REPS	EXERCISES	WEIGHTS/TIME	INTENSITY	NOTES/FEEDBACK

Nutrition Tracker

Breakfast	Dinner
Lunch	Snacks & Drinks

Training Schedule

TYPE	AM TIME	PM TIME	LOCATION

DAILY SWIM TRAINING LOG

Date:　　　　　Location:　　　　　Today's Focus:

Time:　　　　　Pool: 50　25　other　　Coach:

Mood:　　　　　　　　　　　　　　　Day:　M　Tu　W　Th　Fr　Sa　Su

Warm Up

REPS	DISTANCE STROKE/DRILL/KICK	INTERVAL	INTENSITY	NOTES/FEEDBACK

Pre Set

REPS	DISTANCE STROKE/DRILL/KICK	INTERVAL	INTENSITY	NOTES/FEEDBACK

Main Set

REPS	DISTANCE STROKE/DRILL/KICK	INTERVAL	INTENSITY	NOTES/FEEDBACK

Cool Down

Total Distance:　　　　　　　　　　　Total Laps:

©poweredbychlorine.com

Dryland Training

REPS	EXERCISES	WEIGHTS/TIME	INTENSITY	NOTES/FEEDBACK

Nutrition Tracker

Breakfast	Dinner
Lunch	Snacks & Drinks

Training Schedule

TYPE	AM TIME	PM TIME	LOCATION

© poweredbychlorine.com

DAILY SWIM TRAINING LOG

Date: Location: Today's Focus:

Time: Pool: 50   25   other   Coach:

Mood: | Day: M Tu W Th Fr Sa Su

Warm Up

REPS	DISTANCE STROKE/DRILL/KICK	INTERVAL	INTENSITY	NOTES/FEEDBACK

Pre Set

REPS	DISTANCE STROKE/DRILL/KICK	INTERVAL	INTENSITY	NOTES/FEEDBACK

Main Set

REPS	DISTANCE STROKE/DRILL/KICK	INTERVAL	INTENSITY	NOTES/FEEDBACK

Cool Down

Total Distance: Total Laps:

©poweredbychlorine.com

Dryland Training

REPS	EXERCISES	WEIGHTS/TIME	INTENSITY	NOTES/FEEDBACK

Nutrition Tracker

Breakfast	Dinner
Lunch	Snacks & Drinks

Training Schedule

TYPE	AM TIME	PM TIME	LOCATION

DAILY SWIM TRAINING LOG

Date:　　　　　Location:　　　　　Today's Focus:

Time:　　　　　Pool: 50　25　other　　Coach:

Mood: 😀 😀 😀 😀 😀　　　Day:　M　Tu　W　Th　Fr　Sa　Su

Warm Up

REPS	DISTANCE STROKE/DRILL/KICK	INTERVAL	INTENSITY	NOTES/FEEDBACK

Pre Set

REPS	DISTANCE STROKE/DRILL/KICK	INTERVAL	INTENSITY	NOTES/FEEDBACK

Main Set

REPS	DISTANCE STROKE/DRILL/KICK	INTERVAL	INTENSITY	NOTES/FEEDBACK

Cool Down

Total Distance:　　　　　　　　Total Laps:

© poweredbychlorine.com

Dryland Training

REPS	EXERCISES	WEIGHTS/TIME	INTENSITY	NOTES/FEEDBACK

Nutrition Tracker

Breakfast	Dinner
Lunch	Snacks & Drinks

Training Schedule

TYPE	AM TIME	PM TIME	LOCATION

DAILY SWIM TRAINING LOG

Date: Location: Today's Focus:

Time: Pool: 50   25   other   Coach:

Mood: 😀 😀 😀 😀 😀   Day: M   Tu   W   Th   Fr   Sa   Su

Warm Up

REPS	DISTANCE STROKE/DRILL/KICK	INTERVAL	INTENSITY	NOTES/FEEDBACK

Pre Set

REPS	DISTANCE STROKE/DRILL/KICK	INTERVAL	INTENSITY	NOTES/FEEDBACK

Main Set

REPS	DISTANCE STROKE/DRILL/KICK	INTERVAL	INTENSITY	NOTES/FEEDBACK

Cool Down

Total Distance: Total Laps:

©poweredbychlorine.com

Dryland Training

REPS	EXERCISES	WEIGHTS/TIME	INTENSITY	NOTES/FEEDBACK

Nutrition Tracker

Breakfast	Dinner
Lunch	Snacks & Drinks

Training Schedule

TYPE	AM TIME	PM TIME	LOCATION

©poweredbychlorine.com

DAILY SWIM TRAINING LOG

Date:　　　　Location:　　　　　　Today's Focus:

Time:　　　　Pool: 50　25　other　　Coach:

Mood:　　　　　　　　　　　　　　Day:　M　Tu　W　Th　Fr　Sa　Su

Warm Up

REPS	DISTANCE STROKE/DRILL/KICK	INTERVAL	INTENSITY	NOTES/FEEDBACK

Pre Set

REPS	DISTANCE STROKE/DRILL/KICK	INTERVAL	INTENSITY	NOTES/FEEDBACK

Main Set

REPS	DISTANCE STROKE/DRILL/KICK	INTERVAL	INTENSITY	NOTES/FEEDBACK

Cool Down

Total Distance:　　　　　　　　　　Total Laps:

©poweredbychlorine.com

Dryland Training

REPS	EXERCISES	WEIGHTS/TIME	INTENSITY	NOTES/FEEDBACK

Nutrition Tracker

Breakfast	Dinner
Lunch	Snacks & Drinks

Training Schedule

TYPE	AM TIME	PM TIME	LOCATION

©poweredbychlorine.com

DAILY SWIM TRAINING LOG

Date: Location: Today's Focus:

Time: Pool: 50 25 other Coach:

Mood: Day: M Tu W Th Fr Sa Su

Warm Up

REPS	DISTANCE STROKE/DRILL/KICK	INTERVAL	INTENSITY	NOTES/FEEDBACK

Pre Set

REPS	DISTANCE STROKE/DRILL/KICK	INTERVAL	INTENSITY	NOTES/FEEDBACK

Main Set

REPS	DISTANCE STROKE/DRILL/KICK	INTERVAL	INTENSITY	NOTES/FEEDBACK

Cool Down

Total Distance: Total Laps:

©poweredbychlorine.com

Dryland Training

REPS	EXERCISES	WEIGHTS/TIME	INTENSITY	NOTES/FEEDBACK

Nutrition Tracker

Breakfast	Dinner
Lunch	Snacks & Drinks

Training Schedule

TYPE	AM TIME	PM TIME	LOCATION

©poweredbychlorine.com

DAILY SWIM TRAINING LOG

Date: Location: Today's Focus:

Time: Pool: 50   25   other   Coach:

| Mood: | | | | | | Day: | M | Tu | W | Th | Fr | Sa | Su |

Warm Up

REPS	DISTANCE STROKE/DRILL/KICK	INTERVAL	INTENSITY	NOTES/FEEDBACK

Pre Set

REPS	DISTANCE STROKE/DRILL/KICK	INTERVAL	INTENSITY	NOTES/FEEDBACK

Main Set

REPS	DISTANCE STROKE/DRILL/KICK	INTERVAL	INTENSITY	NOTES/FEEDBACK

Cool Down

Total Distance: Total Laps:

©poweredbychlorine.com

Dryland Training

REPS	EXERCISES	WEIGHTS/TIME	INTENSITY	NOTES/FEEDBACK

Nutrition Tracker

Breakfast	Dinner
Lunch	Snacks & Drinks

Training Schedule

TYPE	AM TIME	PM TIME	LOCATION

DAILY SWIM TRAINING LOG

Date: Location: Today's Focus:

Time: Pool: 50   25   other   Coach:

Mood: Day: M   Tu   W   Th   Fr   Sa   Su

Warm Up

REPS	DISTANCE STROKE/DRILL/KICK	INTERVAL	INTENSITY	NOTES/FEEDBACK

Pre Set

REPS	DISTANCE STROKE/DRILL/KICK	INTERVAL	INTENSITY	NOTES/FEEDBACK

Main Set

REPS	DISTANCE STROKE/DRILL/KICK	INTERVAL	INTENSITY	NOTES/FEEDBACK

Cool Down

Total Distance: Total Laps:

©poweredbychlorine.com

Dryland Training

REPS	EXERCISES	WEIGHTS/TIME	INTENSITY	NOTES/FEEDBACK

Nutrition Tracker

Breakfast	Dinner
Lunch	Snacks & Drinks

Training Schedule

TYPE	AM TIME	PM TIME	LOCATION

DAILY SWIM TRAINING LOG

Date: Location: Today's Focus:

Time: Pool: 50   25   other   Coach:

Mood: ⚪⚪⚪⚪⚪   Day: M Tu W Th Fr Sa Su

Warm Up

REPS	DISTANCE STROKE/DRILL/KICK	INTERVAL	INTENSITY	NOTES/FEEDBACK

Pre Set

REPS	DISTANCE STROKE/DRILL/KICK	INTERVAL	INTENSITY	NOTES/FEEDBACK

Main Set

REPS	DISTANCE STROKE/DRILL/KICK	INTERVAL	INTENSITY	NOTES/FEEDBACK

Cool Down

Total Distance: Total Laps:

© poweredbychlorine.com

Dryland Training

REPS	EXERCISES	WEIGHTS/TIME	INTENSITY	NOTES/FEEDBACK

Nutrition Tracker

Breakfast	Dinner
Lunch	Snacks & Drinks

Training Schedule

TYPE	AM TIME	PM TIME	LOCATION

© poweredbychlorine.com

DAILY SWIM TRAINING LOG

Date: Location: Today's Focus:

Time: Pool: 50   25   other   Coach:

Mood: Day: M   Tu   W   Th   Fr   Sa   Su

Warm Up

REPS	DISTANCE STROKE/DRILL/KICK	INTERVAL	INTENSITY	NOTES/FEEDBACK

Pre Set

REPS	DISTANCE STROKE/DRILL/KICK	INTERVAL	INTENSITY	NOTES/FEEDBACK

Main Set

REPS	DISTANCE STROKE/DRILL/KICK	INTERVAL	INTENSITY	NOTES/FEEDBACK

Cool Down

Total Distance: Total Laps:

©poweredbychlorine.com

Dryland Training

REPS	EXERCISES	WEIGHTS/TIME	INTENSITY	NOTES/FEEDBACK

Nutrition Tracker

Breakfast	Dinner
Lunch	Snacks & Drinks

Training Schedule

TYPE	AM TIME	PM TIME	LOCATION

©poweredbychlorine.com

DAILY SWIM TRAINING LOG

Date: Location: Today's Focus:

Time: Pool: 50   25   other Coach:

Mood: Day: M   Tu   W   Th   Fr   Sa   Su

Warm Up

REPS	DISTANCE STROKE/DRILL/KICK	INTERVAL	INTENSITY	NOTES/FEEDBACK

Pre Set

REPS	DISTANCE STROKE/DRILL/KICK	INTERVAL	INTENSITY	NOTES/FEEDBACK

Main Set

REPS	DISTANCE STROKE/DRILL/KICK	INTERVAL	INTENSITY	NOTES/FEEDBACK

Cool Down

Total Distance: Total Laps:

©poweredbychlorine.com

Dryland Training

REPS	EXERCISES	WEIGHTS/TIME	INTENSITY	NOTES/FEEDBACK

Nutrition Tracker

Breakfast	Dinner
Lunch	Snacks & Drinks

Training Schedule

TYPE	AM TIME	PM TIME	LOCATION

©poweredbychlorine.com

DAILY SWIM TRAINING LOG

Date:　　　　　Location:　　　　　　　Today's Focus:

Time:　　　　　Pool: 50　25　other　　Coach:

Mood:　　　　　　　　　　　　　　　Day:　M　Tu　W　Th　Fr　Sa　Su

Warm Up

REPS	DISTANCE STROKE/DRILL/KICK	INTERVAL	INTENSITY	NOTES/FEEDBACK

Pre Set

REPS	DISTANCE STROKE/DRILL/KICK	INTERVAL	INTENSITY	NOTES/FEEDBACK

Main Set

REPS	DISTANCE STROKE/DRILL/KICK	INTERVAL	INTENSITY	NOTES/FEEDBACK

Cool Down

Total Distance:　　　　　　　　　　　Total Laps:

Dryland Training

REPS	EXERCISES	WEIGHTS/TIME	INTENSITY	NOTES/FEEDBACK

Nutrition Tracker

Breakfast	Dinner
Lunch	Snacks & Drinks

Training Schedule

TYPE	AM TIME	PM TIME	LOCATION

©poweredbychlorine.com

DAILY SWIM TRAINING LOG

Date: Location: Today's Focus:

Time: Pool: 50   25   other   Coach:

Mood: Day: M   Tu   W   Th   Fr   Sa   Su

Warm Up

REPS	DISTANCE STROKE/DRILL/KICK	INTERVAL	INTENSITY	NOTES/FEEDBACK

Pre Set

REPS	DISTANCE STROKE/DRILL/KICK	INTERVAL	INTENSITY	NOTES/FEEDBACK

Main Set

REPS	DISTANCE STROKE/DRILL/KICK	INTERVAL	INTENSITY	NOTES/FEEDBACK

Cool Down

Total Distance: Total Laps:

© poweredbychlorine.com

Dryland Training

REPS	EXERCISES	WEIGHTS/TIME	INTENSITY	NOTES/FEEDBACK

Nutrition Tracker

Breakfast	Dinner
Lunch	Snacks & Drinks

Training Schedule

TYPE	AM TIME	PM TIME	LOCATION

DAILY SWIM TRAINING LOG

Date: Location: Today's Focus:

Time: Pool: 50   25   other   Coach:

Mood: Day: M   Tu   W   Th   Fr   Sa   Su

Warm Up

REPS	DISTANCE STROKE/DRILL/KICK	INTERVAL	INTENSITY	NOTES/FEEDBACK

Pre Set

REPS	DISTANCE STROKE/DRILL/KICK	INTERVAL	INTENSITY	NOTES/FEEDBACK

Main Set

REPS	DISTANCE STROKE/DRILL/KICK	INTERVAL	INTENSITY	NOTES/FEEDBACK

Cool Down

Total Distance: Total Laps:

©poweredbychlorine.com

Dryland Training

REPS	EXERCISES	WEIGHTS/TIME	INTENSITY	NOTES/FEEDBACK

Nutrition Tracker

Breakfast	Dinner
Lunch	Snacks & Drinks

Training Schedule

TYPE	AM TIME	PM TIME	LOCATION

DAILY SWIM TRAINING LOG

Date:　　　　　Location:　　　　　Today's Focus:

Time:　　　　　Pool: 50　25　other　　Coach:

Mood:　　　　　　　　　　　　　　　Day:　M　Tu　W　Th　Fr　Sa　Su

Warm Up

REPS	DISTANCE STROKE/DRILL/KICK	INTERVAL	INTENSITY	NOTES/FEEDBACK

Pre Set

REPS	DISTANCE STROKE/DRILL/KICK	INTERVAL	INTENSITY	NOTES/FEEDBACK

Main Set

REPS	DISTANCE STROKE/DRILL/KICK	INTERVAL	INTENSITY	NOTES/FEEDBACK

Cool Down

Total Distance:　　　　　　　　　Total Laps:

Dryland Training

REPS	EXERCISES	WEIGHTS/TIME	INTENSITY	NOTES/FEEDBACK

Nutrition Tracker

Breakfast	Dinner
Lunch	Snacks & Drinks

Training Schedule

TYPE	AM TIME	PM TIME	LOCATION

©poweredbychlorine.com

DAILY SWIM TRAINING LOG

Date: Location: Today's Focus:

Time: Pool: 50   25   other Coach:

Mood: Day: M Tu W Th Fr Sa Su

Warm Up

REPS	DISTANCE STROKE/DRILL/KICK	INTERVAL	INTENSITY	NOTES/FEEDBACK

Pre Set

REPS	DISTANCE STROKE/DRILL/KICK	INTERVAL	INTENSITY	NOTES/FEEDBACK

Main Set

REPS	DISTANCE STROKE/DRILL/KICK	INTERVAL	INTENSITY	NOTES/FEEDBACK

Cool Down

Total Distance: Total Laps:

©poweredbychlorine.com

Dryland Training

REPS	EXERCISES	WEIGHTS/TIME	INTENSITY	NOTES/FEEDBACK

Nutrition Tracker

Breakfast	Dinner
Lunch	Snacks & Drinks

Training Schedule

TYPE	AM TIME	PM TIME	LOCATION

©poweredbychlorine.com

DAILY SWIM TRAINING LOG

Date: Location: Today's Focus:

Time: Pool: 50   25   other   Coach:

Mood: Day: M Tu W Th Fr Sa Su

Warm Up

REPS	DISTANCE STROKE/DRILL/KICK	INTERVAL	INTENSITY	NOTES/FEEDBACK

Pre Set

REPS	DISTANCE STROKE/DRILL/KICK	INTERVAL	INTENSITY	NOTES/FEEDBACK

Main Set

REPS	DISTANCE STROKE/DRILL/KICK	INTERVAL	INTENSITY	NOTES/FEEDBACK

Cool Down

Total Distance: Total Laps:

©poweredbychlorine.com

Dryland Training

REPS	EXERCISES	WEIGHTS/TIME	INTENSITY	NOTES/FEEDBACK

Nutrition Tracker

Breakfast	Dinner
Lunch	Snacks & Drinks

Training Schedule

TYPE	AM TIME	PM TIME	LOCATION

©poweredbychlorine.com

DAILY SWIM TRAINING LOG

Date: Location: Today's Focus:

Time: Pool: 50   25   other   Coach:

Mood: Day: M   Tu   W   Th   Fr   Sa   Su

Warm Up

REPS	DISTANCE STROKE/DRILL/KICK	INTERVAL	INTENSITY	NOTES/FEEDBACK

Pre Set

REPS	DISTANCE STROKE/DRILL/KICK	INTERVAL	INTENSITY	NOTES/FEEDBACK

Main Set

REPS	DISTANCE STROKE/DRILL/KICK	INTERVAL	INTENSITY	NOTES/FEEDBACK

Cool Down

Total Distance: Total Laps:

©poweredbychlorine.com

Dryland Training

REPS	EXERCISES	WEIGHTS/TIME	INTENSITY	NOTES/FEEDBACK

Nutrition Tracker

Breakfast	Dinner
Lunch	Snacks & Drinks

Training Schedule

TYPE	AM TIME	PM TIME	LOCATION

© poweredbychlorine.com

DAILY SWIM TRAINING LOG

Date:　　　　　Location:　　　　　Today's Focus:

Time:　　　　　Pool: 50　25　other　　Coach:

Mood: 😊 😊 😊 😊　　　　　Day:　M　Tu　W　Th　Fr　Sa　Su

Warm Up

REPS	DISTANCE STROKE/DRILL/KICK	INTERVAL	INTENSITY	NOTES/FEEDBACK

Pre Set

REPS	DISTANCE STROKE/DRILL/KICK	INTERVAL	INTENSITY	NOTES/FEEDBACK

Main Set

REPS	DISTANCE STROKE/DRILL/KICK	INTERVAL	INTENSITY	NOTES/FEEDBACK

Cool Down

Total Distance:　　　　　Total Laps:

©poweredbychlorine.com

Dryland Training

REPS	EXERCISES	WEIGHTS/TIME	INTENSITY	NOTES/FEEDBACK

Nutrition Tracker

Breakfast	Dinner
Lunch	Snacks & Drinks

Training Schedule

TYPE	AM TIME	PM TIME	LOCATION

©poweredbychlorine.com

DAILY SWIM TRAINING LOG

Date: Location: Today's Focus:

Time: Pool: 50   25   other   Coach:

Mood: Day: M   Tu   W   Th   Fr   Sa   Su

Warm Up

REPS	DISTANCE STROKE/DRILL/KICK	INTERVAL	INTENSITY	NOTES/FEEDBACK

Pre Set

REPS	DISTANCE STROKE/DRILL/KICK	INTERVAL	INTENSITY	NOTES/FEEDBACK

Main Set

REPS	DISTANCE STROKE/DRILL/KICK	INTERVAL	INTENSITY	NOTES/FEEDBACK

Cool Down

Total Distance: Total Laps:

Dryland Training

REPS	EXERCISES	WEIGHTS/TIME	INTENSITY	NOTES/FEEDBACK

Nutrition Tracker

Breakfast	Dinner
Lunch	Snacks & Drinks

Training Schedule

TYPE	AM TIME	PM TIME	LOCATION

DAILY SWIM TRAINING LOG

Date: Location: Today's Focus:

Time: Pool: 50   25   other   Coach:

Mood: Day: M   Tu   W   Th   Fr   Sa   Su

Warm Up

REPS	DISTANCE STROKE/DRILL/KICK	INTERVAL	INTENSITY	NOTES/FEEDBACK

Pre Set

REPS	DISTANCE STROKE/DRILL/KICK	INTERVAL	INTENSITY	NOTES/FEEDBACK

Main Set

REPS	DISTANCE STROKE/DRILL/KICK	INTERVAL	INTENSITY	NOTES/FEEDBACK

Cool Down

Total Distance: Total Laps:

©poweredbychlorine.com

Dryland Training

REPS	EXERCISES	WEIGHTS/TIME	INTENSITY	NOTES/FEEDBACK

Nutrition Tracker

Breakfast	Dinner
Lunch	Snacks & Drinks

Training Schedule

TYPE	AM TIME	PM TIME	LOCATION

©poweredbychlorine.com

DAILY SWIM TRAINING LOG

Date:　　　　　Location:　　　　　　Today's Focus:

Time:　　　　　Pool: 50　25　other　　Coach:

Mood: ⚫⚫⚫⚫　　　　　　　　　Day:　M　Tu　W　Th　Fr　Sa　Su

Warm Up

REPS	DISTANCE STROKE/DRILL/KICK	INTERVAL	INTENSITY	NOTES/FEEDBACK

Pre Set

REPS	DISTANCE STROKE/DRILL/KICK	INTERVAL	INTENSITY	NOTES/FEEDBACK

Main Set

REPS	DISTANCE STROKE/DRILL/KICK	INTERVAL	INTENSITY	NOTES/FEEDBACK

Cool Down

Total Distance:　　　　　　　　　　　Total Laps:

© poweredbychlorine.com

Dryland Training

REPS	EXERCISES	WEIGHTS/TIME	INTENSITY	NOTES/FEEDBACK

Nutrition Tracker

Breakfast	Dinner
Lunch	Snacks & Drinks

Training Schedule

TYPE	AM TIME	PM TIME	LOCATION

©poweredbychlorine.com

DAILY SWIM TRAINING LOG

Date: Location: Today's Focus:

Time: Pool: 50   25   other Coach:

Mood: Day: M Tu W Th Fr Sa Su

Warm Up

REPS	DISTANCE STROKE/DRILL/KICK	INTERVAL	INTENSITY	NOTES/FEEDBACK

Pre Set

REPS	DISTANCE STROKE/DRILL/KICK	INTERVAL	INTENSITY	NOTES/FEEDBACK

Main Set

REPS	DISTANCE STROKE/DRILL/KICK	INTERVAL	INTENSITY	NOTES/FEEDBACK

Cool Down

Total Distance: Total Laps:

poweredbychlorine.com

Dryland Training

REPS	EXERCISES	WEIGHTS/TIME	INTENSITY	NOTES/FEEDBACK

Nutrition Tracker

Breakfast	Dinner
Lunch	Snacks & Drinks

Training Schedule

TYPE	AM TIME	PM TIME	LOCATION

DAILY SWIM TRAINING LOG

Date: Location: Today's Focus:

Time: Pool: 50   25   other   Coach:

Mood: Day: M   Tu   W   Th   Fr   Sa   Su

Warm Up

REPS	DISTANCE STROKE/DRILL/KICK	INTERVAL	INTENSITY	NOTES/FEEDBACK

Pre Set

REPS	DISTANCE STROKE/DRILL/KICK	INTERVAL	INTENSITY	NOTES/FEEDBACK

Main Set

REPS	DISTANCE STROKE/DRILL/KICK	INTERVAL	INTENSITY	NOTES/FEEDBACK

Cool Down

Total Distance: Total Laps:

©poweredbychlorine.com

Dryland Training

REPS	EXERCISES	WEIGHTS/TIME	INTENSITY	NOTES/FEEDBACK

Nutrition Tracker

Breakfast	Dinner
Lunch	Snacks & Drinks

Training Schedule

TYPE	AM TIME	PM TIME	LOCATION

© poweredbychlorine.com

DAILY SWIM TRAINING LOG

Date: Location: Today's Focus:

Time: Pool: 50   25   other   Coach:

Mood: Day: M   Tu   W   Th   Fr   Sa   Su

Warm Up

REPS	DISTANCE STROKE/DRILL/KICK	INTERVAL	INTENSITY	NOTES/FEEDBACK

Pre Set

REPS	DISTANCE STROKE/DRILL/KICK	INTERVAL	INTENSITY	NOTES/FEEDBACK

Main Set

REPS	DISTANCE STROKE/DRILL/KICK	INTERVAL	INTENSITY	NOTES/FEEDBACK

Cool Down

Total Distance: Total Laps:

©poweredbychlorine.com

Dryland Training

REPS	EXERCISES	WEIGHTS/TIME	INTENSITY	NOTES/FEEDBACK

Nutrition Tracker

Breakfast	Dinner
Lunch	Snacks & Drinks

Training Schedule

TYPE	AM TIME	PM TIME	LOCATION

© poweredbychlorine.com

DAILY SWIM TRAINING LOG

Date: Location: Today's Focus:

Time: Pool: 50   25   other   Coach:

Mood: 😀 😊 😐 😕 😢   Day: M   Tu   W   Th   Fr   Sa   Su

Warm Up

REPS	DISTANCE STROKE/DRILL/KICK	INTERVAL	INTENSITY	NOTES/FEEDBACK

Pre Set

REPS	DISTANCE STROKE/DRILL/KICK	INTERVAL	INTENSITY	NOTES/FEEDBACK

Main Set

REPS	DISTANCE STROKE/DRILL/KICK	INTERVAL	INTENSITY	NOTES/FEEDBACK

Cool Down

Total Distance: Total Laps:

© poweredbychlorine.com

Dryland Training

REPS	EXERCISES	WEIGHTS/TIME	INTENSITY	NOTES/FEEDBACK

Nutrition Tracker

Breakfast	Dinner
Lunch	Snacks & Drinks

Training Schedule

TYPE	AM TIME	PM TIME	LOCATION

©poweredbychlorine.com

DAILY SWIM TRAINING LOG

Date: Location: Today's Focus:

Time: Pool: 50   25   other   Coach:

Mood: Day: M Tu W Th Fr Sa Su

Warm Up

REPS	DISTANCE STROKE/DRILL/KICK	INTERVAL	INTENSITY	NOTES/FEEDBACK

Pre Set

REPS	DISTANCE STROKE/DRILL/KICK	INTERVAL	INTENSITY	NOTES/FEEDBACK

Main Set

REPS	DISTANCE STROKE/DRILL/KICK	INTERVAL	INTENSITY	NOTES/FEEDBACK

Cool Down

Total Distance: Total Laps:

©poweredbychlorine.com

Dryland Training

REPS	EXERCISES	WEIGHTS/TIME	INTENSITY	NOTES/FEEDBACK

Nutrition Tracker

Breakfast	Dinner
Lunch	Snacks & Drinks

Training Schedule

TYPE	AM TIME	PM TIME	LOCATION

DAILY SWIM TRAINING LOG

Date: Location: Today's Focus:

Time: Pool: 50   25   other   Coach:

Mood: Day: M   Tu   W   Th   Fr   Sa   Su

Warm Up

REPS	DISTANCE STROKE/DRILL/KICK	INTERVAL	INTENSITY	NOTES/FEEDBACK

Pre Set

REPS	DISTANCE STROKE/DRILL/KICK	INTERVAL	INTENSITY	NOTES/FEEDBACK

Main Set

REPS	DISTANCE STROKE/DRILL/KICK	INTERVAL	INTENSITY	NOTES/FEEDBACK

Cool Down

Total Distance: Total Laps:

©poweredbychlorine.com

Dryland Training

REPS	EXERCISES	WEIGHTS/TIME	INTENSITY	NOTES/FEEDBACK

Nutrition Tracker

Breakfast	Dinner
Lunch	Snacks & Drinks

Training Schedule

TYPE	AM TIME	PM TIME	LOCATION

© poweredbychlorine.com

DAILY SWIM TRAINING LOG

Date: Location: Today's Focus:

Time: Pool: 50   25   other   Coach:

Mood: Day: M   Tu   W   Th   Fr   Sa   Su

Warm Up

REPS	DISTANCE STROKE/DRILL/KICK	INTERVAL	INTENSITY	NOTES/FEEDBACK

Pre Set

REPS	DISTANCE STROKE/DRILL/KICK	INTERVAL	INTENSITY	NOTES/FEEDBACK

Main Set

REPS	DISTANCE STROKE/DRILL/KICK	INTERVAL	INTENSITY	NOTES/FEEDBACK

Cool Down

Total Distance: Total Laps:

© poweredbychlorine.com

Dryland Training

REPS	EXERCISES	WEIGHTS/TIME	INTENSITY	NOTES/FEEDBACK

Nutrition Tracker

Breakfast	Dinner
Lunch	Snacks & Drinks

Training Schedule

TYPE	AM TIME	PM TIME	LOCATION

DAILY SWIM TRAINING LOG

Date:　　　　　Location:　　　　　　Today's Focus:

Time:　　　　　Pool: 50　　25　　other　　Coach:

Mood:　　　　　　　　　　　　　　　　Day: M　Tu　W　Th　Fr　Sa　Su

Warm Up

REPS	DISTANCE STROKE/DRILL/KICK	INTERVAL	INTENSITY	NOTES/FEEDBACK

Pre Set

REPS	DISTANCE STROKE/DRILL/KICK	INTERVAL	INTENSITY	NOTES/FEEDBACK

Main Set

REPS	DISTANCE STROKE/DRILL/KICK	INTERVAL	INTENSITY	NOTES/FEEDBACK

Cool Down

Total Distance:　　　　　　　　　　Total Laps:

©poweredbychlorine.com

Dryland Training

REPS	EXERCISES	WEIGHTS/TIME	INTENSITY	NOTES/FEEDBACK

Nutrition Tracker

Breakfast	Dinner
Lunch	Snacks & Drinks

Training Schedule

TYPE	AM TIME	PM TIME	LOCATION

©poweredbychlorine.com

DAILY SWIM TRAINING LOG

Date: Location: Today's Focus:

Time: Pool: 50 25 other Coach:

Mood: ☺ ☺ ☺ ☺ ☺ Day: M Tu W Th Fr Sa Su

Warm Up

REPS	DISTANCE STROKE/DRILL/KICK	INTERVAL	INTENSITY	NOTES/FEEDBACK

Pre Set

REPS	DISTANCE STROKE/DRILL/KICK	INTERVAL	INTENSITY	NOTES/FEEDBACK

Main Set

REPS	DISTANCE STROKE/DRILL/KICK	INTERVAL	INTENSITY	NOTES/FEEDBACK

Cool Down

Total Distance: Total Laps:

Dryland Training

REPS	EXERCISES	WEIGHTS/TIME	INTENSITY	NOTES/FEEDBACK

Nutrition Tracker

Breakfast	Dinner
Lunch	Snacks & Drinks

Training Schedule

TYPE	AM TIME	PM TIME	LOCATION

DAILY SWIM TRAINING LOG

Date: Location: Today's Focus:

Time: Pool: 50   25   other Coach:

Mood: Day: M   Tu   W   Th   Fr   Sa   Su

Warm Up

REPS	DISTANCE STROKE/DRILL/KICK	INTERVAL	INTENSITY	NOTES/FEEDBACK

Pre Set

REPS	DISTANCE STROKE/DRILL/KICK	INTERVAL	INTENSITY	NOTES/FEEDBACK

Main Set

REPS	DISTANCE STROKE/DRILL/KICK	INTERVAL	INTENSITY	NOTES/FEEDBACK

Cool Down

Total Distance: Total Laps:

©poweredbychlorine.com

Dryland Training

REPS	EXERCISES	WEIGHTS/TIME	INTENSITY	NOTES/FEEDBACK

Nutrition Tracker

Breakfast	Dinner
Lunch	Snacks & Drinks

Training Schedule

TYPE	AM TIME	PM TIME	LOCATION

DAILY SWIM TRAINING LOG

Date: Location: Today's Focus:

Time: Pool: 50   25   other   Coach:

Mood: Day: M   Tu   W   Th   Fr   Sa   Su

Warm Up

REPS	DISTANCE STROKE/DRILL/KICK	INTERVAL	INTENSITY	NOTES/FEEDBACK

Pre Set

REPS	DISTANCE STROKE/DRILL/KICK	INTERVAL	INTENSITY	NOTES/FEEDBACK

Main Set

REPS	DISTANCE STROKE/DRILL/KICK	INTERVAL	INTENSITY	NOTES/FEEDBACK

Cool Down

Total Distance: Total Laps:

©poweredbychlorine.com

Dryland Training

REPS	EXERCISES	WEIGHTS/TIME	INTENSITY	NOTES/FEEDBACK

Nutrition Tracker

Breakfast	Dinner
Lunch	Snacks & Drinks

Training Schedule

TYPE	AM TIME	PM TIME	LOCATION

© poweredbychlorine.com

DAILY SWIM TRAINING LOG

Date: Location: Today's Focus:

Time: Pool: 50   25   other   Coach:

Mood: Day: M   Tu   W   Th   Fr   Sa   Su

Warm Up

REPS	DISTANCE STROKE/DRILL/KICK	INTERVAL	INTENSITY	NOTES/FEEDBACK

Pre Set

REPS	DISTANCE STROKE/DRILL/KICK	INTERVAL	INTENSITY	NOTES/FEEDBACK

Main Set

REPS	DISTANCE STROKE/DRILL/KICK	INTERVAL	INTENSITY	NOTES/FEEDBACK

Cool Down

Total Distance: Total Laps:

©poweredbychlorine.com

Dryland Training

REPS	EXERCISES	WEIGHTS/TIME	INTENSITY	NOTES/FEEDBACK

Nutrition Tracker

Breakfast	Dinner
Lunch	Snacks & Drinks

Training Schedule

TYPE	AM TIME	PM TIME	LOCATION

©poweredbychlorine.com

DAILY SWIM TRAINING LOG

Date: Location: Today's Focus:

Time: Pool: 50   25   other   Coach:

Mood: 😐 😐 😐 😐 😐   Day: M Tu W Th Fr Sa Su

Warm Up

REPS	DISTANCE STROKE/DRILL/KICK	INTERVAL	INTENSITY	NOTES/FEEDBACK

Pre Set

REPS	DISTANCE STROKE/DRILL/KICK	INTERVAL	INTENSITY	NOTES/FEEDBACK

Main Set

REPS	DISTANCE STROKE/DRILL/KICK	INTERVAL	INTENSITY	NOTES/FEEDBACK

Cool Down

Total Distance: Total Laps:

© poweredbychlorine.com

Dryland Training

REPS	EXERCISES	WEIGHTS/TIME	INTENSITY	NOTES/FEEDBACK

Nutrition Tracker

Breakfast	Dinner
Lunch	Snacks & Drinks

Training Schedule

TYPE	AM TIME	PM TIME	LOCATION

©poweredbychlorine.com

DAILY SWIM TRAINING LOG

Date: Location: Today's Focus:

Time: Pool: 50   25   other   Coach:

| Mood: | | Day: M Tu W Th Fr Sa Su |

Warm Up

REPS	DISTANCE STROKE/DRILL/KICK	INTERVAL	INTENSITY	NOTES/FEEDBACK

Pre Set

REPS	DISTANCE STROKE/DRILL/KICK	INTERVAL	INTENSITY	NOTES/FEEDBACK

Main Set

REPS	DISTANCE STROKE/DRILL/KICK	INTERVAL	INTENSITY	NOTES/FEEDBACK

Cool Down

Total Distance: Total Laps:

©poweredbychlorine.com

Dryland Training

REPS	EXERCISES	WEIGHTS/TIME	INTENSITY	NOTES/FEEDBACK

Nutrition Tracker

Breakfast	Dinner
Lunch	Snacks & Drinks

Training Schedule

TYPE	AM TIME	PM TIME	LOCATION

DAILY SWIM TRAINING LOG

Date: Location: Today's Focus:

Time: Pool: 50 25 other Coach:

Mood: Day: M Tu W Th Fr Sa Su

Warm Up

REPS	DISTANCE STROKE/DRILL/KICK	INTERVAL	INTENSITY	NOTES/FEEDBACK

Pre Set

REPS	DISTANCE STROKE/DRILL/KICK	INTERVAL	INTENSITY	NOTES/FEEDBACK

Main Set

REPS	DISTANCE STROKE/DRILL/KICK	INTERVAL	INTENSITY	NOTES/FEEDBACK

Cool Down

Total Distance: Total Laps:

©poweredbychlorine.com

Dryland Training

REPS	EXERCISES	WEIGHTS/TIME	INTENSITY	NOTES/FEEDBACK

Nutrition Tracker

Breakfast	Dinner
Lunch	Snacks & Drinks

Training Schedule

TYPE	AM TIME	PM TIME	LOCATION

DAILY SWIM TRAINING LOG

Date: Location: Today's Focus:

Time: Pool: 50   25   other   Coach:

Mood: ☺ ☺ ☺ ☺ ☺   Day: M   Tu   W   Th   Fr   Sa   Su

Warm Up

REPS	DISTANCE STROKE/DRILL/KICK	INTERVAL	INTENSITY	NOTES/FEEDBACK

Pre Set

REPS	DISTANCE STROKE/DRILL/KICK	INTERVAL	INTENSITY	NOTES/FEEDBACK

Main Set

REPS	DISTANCE STROKE/DRILL/KICK	INTERVAL	INTENSITY	NOTES/FEEDBACK

Cool Down

Total Distance: Total Laps:

©poweredbychlorine.com

Dryland Training

REPS	EXERCISES	WEIGHTS/TIME	INTENSITY	NOTES/FEEDBACK

Nutrition Tracker

Breakfast	Dinner
Lunch	Snacks & Drinks

Training Schedule

TYPE	AM TIME	PM TIME	LOCATION

DAILY SWIM TRAINING LOG

Date: Location: Today's Focus:

Time: Pool: 50 25 other Coach:

Mood: Day: M Tu W Th Fr Sa Su

Warm Up

REPS	DISTANCE STROKE/DRILL/KICK	INTERVAL	INTENSITY	NOTES/FEEDBACK

Pre Set

REPS	DISTANCE STROKE/DRILL/KICK	INTERVAL	INTENSITY	NOTES/FEEDBACK

Main Set

REPS	DISTANCE STROKE/DRILL/KICK	INTERVAL	INTENSITY	NOTES/FEEDBACK

Cool Down

Total Distance: Total Laps:

© poweredbychlorine.com

Dryland Training

REPS	EXERCISES	WEIGHTS/TIME	INTENSITY	NOTES/FEEDBACK

Nutrition Tracker

Breakfast	Dinner
Lunch	Snacks & Drinks

Training Schedule

TYPE	AM TIME	PM TIME	LOCATION

©poweredbychlorine.com

DAILY SWIM TRAINING LOG

Date: Location: Today's Focus:

Time: Pool: 50   25   other   Coach:

Mood: Day: M   Tu   W   Th   Fr   Sa   Su

Warm Up

REPS	DISTANCE STROKE/DRILL/KICK	INTERVAL	INTENSITY	NOTES/FEEDBACK

Pre Set

REPS	DISTANCE STROKE/DRILL/KICK	INTERVAL	INTENSITY	NOTES/FEEDBACK

Main Set

REPS	DISTANCE STROKE/DRILL/KICK	INTERVAL	INTENSITY	NOTES/FEEDBACK

Cool Down

Total Distance: Total Laps:

©poweredbychlorine.com

Dryland Training

REPS	EXERCISES	WEIGHTS/TIME	INTENSITY	NOTES/FEEDBACK

Nutrition Tracker

Breakfast	Dinner
Lunch	Snacks & Drinks

Training Schedule

TYPE	AM TIME	PM TIME	LOCATION

© poweredbychlorine.com

DAILY SWIM TRAINING LOG

Date: Location: Today's Focus:

Time: Pool: 50   25   other   Coach:

Mood: 😀 😀 😀 😀 😀   Day: M Tu W Th Fr Sa Su

Warm Up

REPS	DISTANCE STROKE/DRILL/KICK	INTERVAL	INTENSITY	NOTES/FEEDBACK

Pre Set

REPS	DISTANCE STROKE/DRILL/KICK	INTERVAL	INTENSITY	NOTES/FEEDBACK

Main Set

REPS	DISTANCE STROKE/DRILL/KICK	INTERVAL	INTENSITY	NOTES/FEEDBACK

Cool Down

Total Distance: Total Laps:

©poweredbychlorine.com

Dryland Training

REPS	EXERCISES	WEIGHTS/TIME	INTENSITY	NOTES/FEEDBACK

Nutrition Tracker

Breakfast	Dinner
Lunch	Snacks & Drinks

Training Schedule

TYPE	AM TIME	PM TIME	LOCATION

©poweredbychlorine.com

DAILY SWIM TRAINING LOG

Date:　　　　　Location:　　　　　　Today's Focus:

Time:　　　　　Pool: 50　25　other　　Coach:

Mood:　　　　　　　　　　　　　　　Day:　M　Tu　W　Th　Fr　Sa　Su

Warm Up

REPS	DISTANCE STROKE/DRILL/KICK	INTERVAL	INTENSITY	NOTES/FEEDBACK

Pre Set

REPS	DISTANCE STROKE/DRILL/KICK	INTERVAL	INTENSITY	NOTES/FEEDBACK

Main Set

REPS	DISTANCE STROKE/DRILL/KICK	INTERVAL	INTENSITY	NOTES/FEEDBACK

Cool Down

Total Distance:　　　　　　　　　　　Total Laps:

©poweredbychlorine.com

Dryland Training

REPS	EXERCISES	WEIGHTS/TIME	INTENSITY	NOTES/FEEDBACK

Nutrition Tracker

Breakfast	Dinner
Lunch	Snacks & Drinks

Training Schedule

TYPE	AM TIME	PM TIME	LOCATION

© poweredbychlorine.com

DAILY SWIM TRAINING LOG

Date: Location: Today's Focus:

Time: Pool: 50   25   other   Coach:

Mood: 😀 😊 😐 😕 😢   Day: M Tu W Th Fr Sa Su

Warm Up

REPS	DISTANCE STROKE/DRILL/KICK	INTERVAL	INTENSITY	NOTES/FEEDBACK

Pre Set

REPS	DISTANCE STROKE/DRILL/KICK	INTERVAL	INTENSITY	NOTES/FEEDBACK

Main Set

REPS	DISTANCE STROKE/DRILL/KICK	INTERVAL	INTENSITY	NOTES/FEEDBACK

Cool Down

Total Distance: Total Laps:

© poweredbychlorine.com

Dryland Training

REPS	EXERCISES	WEIGHTS/TIME	INTENSITY	NOTES/FEEDBACK

Nutrition Tracker

Breakfast	Dinner
Lunch	Snacks & Drinks

Training Schedule

TYPE	AM TIME	PM TIME	LOCATION

© poweredbychlorine.com

DAILY SWIM TRAINING LOG

Date: Location: Today's Focus:

Time: Pool: 50   25   other   Coach:

Mood: Day: M   Tu   W   Th   Fr   Sa   Su

Warm Up

REPS	DISTANCE STROKE/DRILL/KICK	INTERVAL	INTENSITY	NOTES/FEEDBACK

Pre Set

REPS	DISTANCE STROKE/DRILL/KICK	INTERVAL	INTENSITY	NOTES/FEEDBACK

Main Set

REPS	DISTANCE STROKE/DRILL/KICK	INTERVAL	INTENSITY	NOTES/FEEDBACK

Cool Down

Total Distance: Total Laps:

©poweredbychlorine.com

Dryland Training

REPS	EXERCISES	WEIGHTS/TIME	INTENSITY	NOTES/FEEDBACK

Nutrition Tracker

Breakfast	Dinner
Lunch	Snacks & Drinks

Training Schedule

TYPE	AM TIME	PM TIME	LOCATION

©poweredbychlorine.com

DAILY SWIM TRAINING LOG

Date: Location: Today's Focus:

Time: Pool: 50 25 other Coach:

Mood: Day: M Tu W Th Fr Sa Su

Warm Up

REPS	DISTANCE STROKE/DRILL/KICK	INTERVAL	INTENSITY	NOTES/FEEDBACK

Pre Set

REPS	DISTANCE STROKE/DRILL/KICK	INTERVAL	INTENSITY	NOTES/FEEDBACK

Main Set

REPS	DISTANCE STROKE/DRILL/KICK	INTERVAL	INTENSITY	NOTES/FEEDBACK

Cool Down

Total Distance: Total Laps:

©poweredbychlorine.com

Dryland Training

REPS	EXERCISES	WEIGHTS/TIME	INTENSITY	NOTES/FEEDBACK

Nutrition Tracker

Breakfast	Dinner
Lunch	Snacks & Drinks

Training Schedule

TYPE	AM TIME	PM TIME	LOCATION

DAILY SWIM TRAINING LOG

Date: Location: Today's Focus:

Time: Pool: 50   25   other   Coach:

Mood: Day: M Tu W Th Fr Sa Su

Warm Up

REPS	DISTANCE STROKE/DRILL/KICK	INTERVAL	INTENSITY	NOTES/FEEDBACK

Pre Set

REPS	DISTANCE STROKE/DRILL/KICK	INTERVAL	INTENSITY	NOTES/FEEDBACK

Main Set

REPS	DISTANCE STROKE/DRILL/KICK	INTERVAL	INTENSITY	NOTES/FEEDBACK

Cool Down

Total Distance: Total Laps:

©poweredbychlorine.com

Dryland Training

REPS	EXERCISES	WEIGHTS/TIME	INTENSITY	NOTES/FEEDBACK

Nutrition Tracker

Breakfast	Dinner
Lunch	Snacks & Drinks

Training Schedule

TYPE	AM TIME	PM TIME	LOCATION

©poweredbychlorine.com

DAILY SWIM TRAINING LOG

Date: Location: Today's Focus:

Time: Pool: 50   25   other   Coach:

Mood: Day: M   Tu   W   Th   Fr   Sa   Su

Warm Up

REPS	DISTANCE STROKE/DRILL/KICK	INTERVAL	INTENSITY	NOTES/FEEDBACK

Pre Set

REPS	DISTANCE STROKE/DRILL/KICK	INTERVAL	INTENSITY	NOTES/FEEDBACK

Main Set

REPS	DISTANCE STROKE/DRILL/KICK	INTERVAL	INTENSITY	NOTES/FEEDBACK

Cool Down

Total Distance: Total Laps:

© poweredbychlorine.com

Dryland Training

REPS	EXERCISES	WEIGHTS/TIME	INTENSITY	NOTES/FEEDBACK

Nutrition Tracker

Breakfast	Dinner
Lunch	Snacks & Drinks

Training Schedule

TYPE	AM TIME	PM TIME	LOCATION

©poweredbychlorine.com

DAILY SWIM TRAINING LOG

Date: Location: Today's Focus:

Time: Pool: 50   25   other Coach:

Mood: 😀 😀 😀 😀 😀   Day: M Tu W Th Fr Sa Su

Warm Up

REPS	DISTANCE STROKE/DRILL/KICK	INTERVAL	INTENSITY	NOTES/FEEDBACK

Pre Set

REPS	DISTANCE STROKE/DRILL/KICK	INTERVAL	INTENSITY	NOTES/FEEDBACK

Main Set

REPS	DISTANCE STROKE/DRILL/KICK	INTERVAL	INTENSITY	NOTES/FEEDBACK

Cool Down

Total Distance: Total Laps:

©poweredbychlorine.com

Dryland Training

REPS	EXERCISES	WEIGHTS/TIME	INTENSITY	NOTES/FEEDBACK

Nutrition Tracker

Breakfast	Dinner
Lunch	Snacks & Drinks

Training Schedule

TYPE	AM TIME	PM TIME	LOCATION

© poweredbychlorine.com

DAILY SWIM TRAINING LOG

Date: Location: Today's Focus:

Time: Pool: 50 25 other Coach:

Mood: 😀 😀 😀 😀 Day: M Tu W Th Fr Sa Su

Warm Up

REPS	DISTANCE STROKE/DRILL/KICK	INTERVAL	INTENSITY	NOTES/FEEDBACK

Pre Set

REPS	DISTANCE STROKE/DRILL/KICK	INTERVAL	INTENSITY	NOTES/FEEDBACK

Main Set

REPS	DISTANCE STROKE/DRILL/KICK	INTERVAL	INTENSITY	NOTES/FEEDBACK

Cool Down

Total Distance: Total Laps:

© poweredbychlorine.com

Dryland Training

REPS	EXERCISES	WEIGHTS/TIME	INTENSITY	NOTES/FEEDBACK

Nutrition Tracker

Breakfast	Dinner
Lunch	Snacks & Drinks

Training Schedule

TYPE	AM TIME	PM TIME	LOCATION

DAILY SWIM TRAINING LOG

Date: Location: Today's Focus:

Time: Pool: 50   25   other   Coach:

Mood: Day: M   Tu   W   Th   Fr   Sa   Su

Warm Up

REPS	DISTANCE STROKE/DRILL/KICK	INTERVAL	INTENSITY	NOTES/FEEDBACK

Pre Set

REPS	DISTANCE STROKE/DRILL/KICK	INTERVAL	INTENSITY	NOTES/FEEDBACK

Main Set

REPS	DISTANCE STROKE/DRILL/KICK	INTERVAL	INTENSITY	NOTES/FEEDBACK

Cool Down

Total Distance: Total Laps:

©poweredbychlorine.com

Dryland Training

REPS	EXERCISES	WEIGHTS/TIME	INTENSITY	NOTES/FEEDBACK

Nutrition Tracker

Breakfast	Dinner
Lunch	Snacks & Drinks

Training Schedule

TYPE	AM TIME	PM TIME	LOCATION

© poweredbychlorine.com

DAILY SWIM TRAINING LOG

Date: Location: Today's Focus:

Time: Pool: 50   25   other   Coach:

Mood: Day: M   Tu   W   Th   Fr   Sa   Su

Warm Up

REPS	DISTANCE STROKE/DRILL/KICK	INTERVAL	INTENSITY	NOTES/FEEDBACK

Pre Set

REPS	DISTANCE STROKE/DRILL/KICK	INTERVAL	INTENSITY	NOTES/FEEDBACK

Main Set

REPS	DISTANCE STROKE/DRILL/KICK	INTERVAL	INTENSITY	NOTES/FEEDBACK

Cool Down

Total Distance: Total Laps:

©poweredbychlorine.com

Dryland Training

REPS	EXERCISES	WEIGHTS/TIME	INTENSITY	NOTES/FEEDBACK

Nutrition Tracker

Breakfast	Dinner
Lunch	Snacks & Drinks

Training Schedule

TYPE	AM TIME	PM TIME	LOCATION

© poweredbychlorine.com

DAILY SWIM TRAINING LOG

Date: Location: Today's Focus:

Time: Pool: 50   25   other   Coach:

Mood: Day: M   Tu   W   Th   Fr   Sa   Su

Warm Up

REPS	DISTANCE STROKE/DRILL/KICK	INTERVAL	INTENSITY	NOTES/FEEDBACK

Pre Set

REPS	DISTANCE STROKE/DRILL/KICK	INTERVAL	INTENSITY	NOTES/FEEDBACK

Main Set

REPS	DISTANCE STROKE/DRILL/KICK	INTERVAL	INTENSITY	NOTES/FEEDBACK

Cool Down

Total Distance: Total Laps:

©poweredbychlorine.com

Dryland Training

REPS	EXERCISES	WEIGHTS/TIME	INTENSITY	NOTES/FEEDBACK

Nutrition Tracker

Breakfast	Dinner
Lunch	Snacks & Drinks

Training Schedule

TYPE	AM TIME	PM TIME	LOCATION

DAILY SWIM TRAINING LOG

Date:　　　　　Location:　　　　　　Today's Focus:

Time:　　　　　Pool: 50　25　other　　Coach:

Mood:　　　　　　　　　　　　　Day:　M　Tu　W　Th　Fr　Sa　Su

Warm Up

REPS	DISTANCE STROKE/DRILL/KICK	INTERVAL	INTENSITY	NOTES/FEEDBACK

Pre Set

REPS	DISTANCE STROKE/DRILL/KICK	INTERVAL	INTENSITY	NOTES/FEEDBACK

Main Set

REPS	DISTANCE STROKE/DRILL/KICK	INTERVAL	INTENSITY	NOTES/FEEDBACK

Cool Down

Total Distance:　　　　　　　　　Total Laps:

©poweredbychlorine.com

Dryland Training

REPS	EXERCISES	WEIGHTS/TIME	INTENSITY	NOTES/FEEDBACK

Nutrition Tracker

Breakfast	Dinner
Lunch	Snacks & Drinks

Training Schedule

TYPE	AM TIME	PM TIME	LOCATION

©poweredbychlorine.com

DAILY SWIM TRAINING LOG

Date: Location: Today's Focus:

Time: Pool: 50 25 other Coach:

Mood: Day: M Tu W Th Fr Sa Su

Warm Up

REPS	DISTANCE STROKE/DRILL/KICK	INTERVAL	INTENSITY	NOTES/FEEDBACK

Pre Set

REPS	DISTANCE STROKE/DRILL/KICK	INTERVAL	INTENSITY	NOTES/FEEDBACK

Main Set

REPS	DISTANCE STROKE/DRILL/KICK	INTERVAL	INTENSITY	NOTES/FEEDBACK

Cool Down

Total Distance: Total Laps:

©poweredbychlorine.com

Dryland Training

REPS	EXERCISES	WEIGHTS/TIME	INTENSITY	NOTES/FEEDBACK

Nutrition Tracker

Breakfast	Dinner
Lunch	Snacks & Drinks

Training Schedule

TYPE	AM TIME	PM TIME	LOCATION

©poweredbychlorine.com

DAILY SWIM TRAINING LOG

Date: Location: Today's Focus:

Time: Pool: 50   25   other   Coach:

Mood: Day: M   Tu   W   Th   Fr   Sa   Su

Warm Up

REPS	DISTANCE STROKE/DRILL/KICK	INTERVAL	INTENSITY	NOTES/FEEDBACK

Pre Set

REPS	DISTANCE STROKE/DRILL/KICK	INTERVAL	INTENSITY	NOTES/FEEDBACK

Main Set

REPS	DISTANCE STROKE/DRILL/KICK	INTERVAL	INTENSITY	NOTES/FEEDBACK

Cool Down

Total Distance: Total Laps:

© poweredbychlorine.com

Dryland Training

REPS	EXERCISES	WEIGHTS/TIME	INTENSITY	NOTES/FEEDBACK

Nutrition Tracker

Breakfast	Dinner
Lunch	Snacks & Drinks

Training Schedule

TYPE	AM TIME	PM TIME	LOCATION

DAILY SWIM TRAINING LOG

Date:　　　　Location:　　　　　　Today's Focus:

Time:　　　　Pool: 50　25　other　　Coach:

Mood:　　　　　　　　　　　　Day:　M　Tu　W　Th　Fr　Sa　Su

Warm Up

REPS	DISTANCE STROKE/DRILL/KICK	INTERVAL	INTENSITY	NOTES/FEEDBACK

Pre Set

REPS	DISTANCE STROKE/DRILL/KICK	INTERVAL	INTENSITY	NOTES/FEEDBACK

Main Set

REPS	DISTANCE STROKE/DRILL/KICK	INTERVAL	INTENSITY	NOTES/FEEDBACK

Cool Down

Total Distance:　　　　　　　　　　　Total Laps:

© poweredbychlorine.com

Dryland Training

REPS	EXERCISES	WEIGHTS/TIME	INTENSITY	NOTES/FEEDBACK

Nutrition Tracker

Breakfast	Dinner
Lunch	Snacks & Drinks

Training Schedule

TYPE	AM TIME	PM TIME	LOCATION

©poweredbychlorine.com

DAILY SWIM TRAINING LOG

Date: Location: Today's Focus:

Time: Pool: 50   25   other   Coach:

Mood: ☺ ☺ ☺ ☺ ☺   Day: M   Tu   W   Th   Fr   Sa   Su

Warm Up

REPS	DISTANCE STROKE/DRILL/KICK	INTERVAL	INTENSITY	NOTES/FEEDBACK

Pre Set

REPS	DISTANCE STROKE/DRILL/KICK	INTERVAL	INTENSITY	NOTES/FEEDBACK

Main Set

REPS	DISTANCE STROKE/DRILL/KICK	INTERVAL	INTENSITY	NOTES/FEEDBACK

Cool Down

Total Distance: Total Laps:

©poweredbychlorine.com

Dryland Training

REPS	EXERCISES	WEIGHTS/TIME	INTENSITY	NOTES/FEEDBACK

Nutrition Tracker

Breakfast	Dinner
Lunch	Snacks & Drinks

Training Schedule

TYPE	AM TIME	PM TIME	LOCATION

DAILY SWIM TRAINING LOG

Date:　　　　　Location:　　　　　Today's Focus:

Time:　　　　　Pool: 50　25　other　　Coach:

| Mood: 😊 😊 😊 😊 😊 | Day: | M | Tu | W | Th | Fr | Sa | Su |

Warm Up

REPS	DISTANCE STROKE/DRILL/KICK	INTERVAL	INTENSITY	NOTES/FEEDBACK

Pre Set

REPS	DISTANCE STROKE/DRILL/KICK	INTERVAL	INTENSITY	NOTES/FEEDBACK

Main Set

REPS	DISTANCE STROKE/DRILL/KICK	INTERVAL	INTENSITY	NOTES/FEEDBACK

Cool Down

Total Distance:　　　　　　　　　　　Total Laps:

© poweredbychlorine.com

Dryland Training

REPS	EXERCISES	WEIGHTS/TIME	INTENSITY	NOTES/FEEDBACK

Nutrition Tracker

Breakfast	Dinner
Lunch	Snacks & Drinks

Training Schedule

TYPE	AM TIME	PM TIME	LOCATION

© poweredbychlorine.com

DAILY SWIM TRAINING LOG

Date:　　　　　Location:　　　　　Today's Focus:

Time:　　　　　Pool: 50　25　other　　Coach:

Mood:　　　　　　　　　　　　　　　Day:　M　Tu　W　Th　Fr　Sa　Su

Warm Up

REPS	DISTANCE STROKE/DRILL/KICK	INTERVAL	INTENSITY	NOTES/FEEDBACK

Pre Set

REPS	DISTANCE STROKE/DRILL/KICK	INTERVAL	INTENSITY	NOTES/FEEDBACK

Main Set

REPS	DISTANCE STROKE/DRILL/KICK	INTERVAL	INTENSITY	NOTES/FEEDBACK

Cool Down

Total Distance:　　　　　　　　　　　Total Laps:

© poweredbychlorine.com

Dryland Training

REPS	EXERCISES	WEIGHTS/TIME	INTENSITY	NOTES/FEEDBACK

Nutrition Tracker

Breakfast	Dinner
Lunch	Snacks & Drinks

Training Schedule

TYPE	AM TIME	PM TIME	LOCATION

© poweredbychlorine.com

DAILY SWIM TRAINING LOG

Date:　　　　　Location:　　　　　Today's Focus:

Time:　　　　　Pool: 50　25　other　　Coach:

Mood:　　　　　　　　　　　　　　　Day:　M　Tu　W　Th　Fr　Sa　Su

Warm Up

REPS	DISTANCE STROKE/DRILL/KICK	INTERVAL	INTENSITY	NOTES/FEEDBACK

Pre Set

REPS	DISTANCE STROKE/DRILL/KICK	INTERVAL	INTENSITY	NOTES/FEEDBACK

Main Set

REPS	DISTANCE STROKE/DRILL/KICK	INTERVAL	INTENSITY	NOTES/FEEDBACK

Cool Down

Total Distance:　　　　　　　　　　　Total Laps:

©poweredbychlorine.com

Dryland Training

REPS	EXERCISES	WEIGHTS/TIME	INTENSITY	NOTES/FEEDBACK

Nutrition Tracker

Breakfast	Dinner
Lunch	Snacks & Drinks

Training Schedule

TYPE	AM TIME	PM TIME	LOCATION

DAILY SWIM TRAINING LOG

Date: Location: Today's Focus:

Time: Pool: 50 25 other Coach:

Mood: ☺ ☺ ☺ ☺ ☺   Day: M Tu W Th Fr Sa Su

Warm Up

REPS	DISTANCE STROKE/DRILL/KICK	INTERVAL	INTENSITY	NOTES/FEEDBACK

Pre Set

REPS	DISTANCE STROKE/DRILL/KICK	INTERVAL	INTENSITY	NOTES/FEEDBACK

Main Set

REPS	DISTANCE STROKE/DRILL/KICK	INTERVAL	INTENSITY	NOTES/FEEDBACK

Cool Down

Total Distance: Total Laps:

Dryland Training

REPS	EXERCISES	WEIGHTS/TIME	INTENSITY	NOTES/FEEDBACK

Nutrition Tracker

Breakfast	Dinner
Lunch	Snacks & Drinks

Training Schedule

TYPE	AM TIME	PM TIME	LOCATION

DAILY SWIM TRAINING LOG

Date: Location: Today's Focus:

Time: Pool: 50   25   other   Coach:

Mood: Day: M Tu W Th Fr Sa Su

Warm Up

REPS	DISTANCE STROKE/DRILL/KICK	INTERVAL	INTENSITY	NOTES/FEEDBACK

Pre Set

REPS	DISTANCE STROKE/DRILL/KICK	INTERVAL	INTENSITY	NOTES/FEEDBACK

Main Set

REPS	DISTANCE STROKE/DRILL/KICK	INTERVAL	INTENSITY	NOTES/FEEDBACK

Cool Down

Total Distance: Total Laps:

©poweredbychlorine.com

Dryland Training

REPS	EXERCISES	WEIGHTS/TIME	INTENSITY	NOTES/FEEDBACK

Nutrition Tracker

Breakfast	Dinner
Lunch	Snacks & Drinks

Training Schedule

TYPE	AM TIME	PM TIME	LOCATION

©poweredbychlorine.com

DAILY SWIM TRAINING LOG

Date: Location: Today's Focus:

Time: Pool: 50   25   other   Coach:

Mood: Day: M   Tu   W   Th   Fr   Sa   Su

Warm Up

REPS	DISTANCE STROKE/DRILL/KICK	INTERVAL	INTENSITY	NOTES/FEEDBACK

Pre Set

REPS	DISTANCE STROKE/DRILL/KICK	INTERVAL	INTENSITY	NOTES/FEEDBACK

Main Set

REPS	DISTANCE STROKE/DRILL/KICK	INTERVAL	INTENSITY	NOTES/FEEDBACK

Cool Down

Total Distance: Total Laps:

Dryland Training

REPS	EXERCISES	WEIGHTS/TIME	INTENSITY	NOTES/FEEDBACK

Nutrition Tracker

Breakfast	Dinner
Lunch	Snacks & Drinks

Training Schedule

TYPE	AM TIME	PM TIME	LOCATION

©poweredbychlorine.com

DAILY SWIM TRAINING LOG

Date: Location: Today's Focus:

Time: Pool: 50   25   other   Coach:

Mood: Day: M   Tu   W   Th   Fr   Sa   Su

Warm Up

REPS	DISTANCE STROKE/DRILL/KICK	INTERVAL	INTENSITY	NOTES/FEEDBACK

Pre Set

REPS	DISTANCE STROKE/DRILL/KICK	INTERVAL	INTENSITY	NOTES/FEEDBACK

Main Set

REPS	DISTANCE STROKE/DRILL/KICK	INTERVAL	INTENSITY	NOTES/FEEDBACK

Cool Down

Total Distance: Total Laps:

© poweredbychlorine.com

Dryland Training

REPS	EXERCISES	WEIGHTS/TIME	INTENSITY	NOTES/FEEDBACK

Nutrition Tracker

Breakfast	Dinner
Lunch	Snacks & Drinks

Training Schedule

TYPE	AM TIME	PM TIME	LOCATION

DAILY SWIM TRAINING LOG

Date:　　　　　Location:　　　　　Today's Focus:

Time:　　　　　Pool: 50　25　other　　Coach:

Mood:　　　　　　　　　　　　　　　Day:　M　Tu　W　Th　Fr　Sa　Su

Warm Up

REPS	DISTANCE STROKE/DRILL/KICK	INTERVAL	INTENSITY	NOTES/FEEDBACK

Pre Set

REPS	DISTANCE STROKE/DRILL/KICK	INTERVAL	INTENSITY	NOTES/FEEDBACK

Main Set

REPS	DISTANCE STROKE/DRILL/KICK	INTERVAL	INTENSITY	NOTES/FEEDBACK

Cool Down

Total Distance:　　　　　　　　　　Total Laps:

© poweredbychlorine.com

Dryland Training

REPS	EXERCISES	WEIGHTS/TIME	INTENSITY	NOTES/FEEDBACK

Nutrition Tracker

Breakfast	Dinner
Lunch	Snacks & Drinks

Training Schedule

TYPE	AM TIME	PM TIME	LOCATION

©poweredbychlorine.com

DAILY SWIM TRAINING LOG

Date:　　　　　Location:　　　　　Today's Focus:

Time:　　　　　Pool: 50　25　other　　Coach:

Mood:　　　　　　　　　　　　　　Day:　M　Tu　W　Th　Fr　Sa　Su

Warm Up

REPS	DISTANCE STROKE/DRILL/KICK	INTERVAL	INTENSITY	NOTES/FEEDBACK

Pre Set

REPS	DISTANCE STROKE/DRILL/KICK	INTERVAL	INTENSITY	NOTES/FEEDBACK

Main Set

REPS	DISTANCE STROKE/DRILL/KICK	INTERVAL	INTENSITY	NOTES/FEEDBACK

Cool Down

Total Distance:　　　　　　　　　　　　　　Total Laps:

© poweredbychlorine.com

Dryland Training

REPS	EXERCISES	WEIGHTS/TIME	INTENSITY	NOTES/FEEDBACK

Nutrition Tracker

Breakfast	Dinner
Lunch	Snacks & Drinks

Training Schedule

TYPE	AM TIME	PM TIME	LOCATION

©poweredbychlorine.com

DAILY SWIM TRAINING LOG

Date: Location: Today's Focus:

Time: Pool: 50 25 other   Coach:

Mood: Day: M Tu W Th Fr Sa Su

Warm Up

REPS	DISTANCE STROKE/DRILL/KICK	INTERVAL	INTENSITY	NOTES/FEEDBACK

Pre Set

REPS	DISTANCE STROKE/DRILL/KICK	INTERVAL	INTENSITY	NOTES/FEEDBACK

Main Set

REPS	DISTANCE STROKE/DRILL/KICK	INTERVAL	INTENSITY	NOTES/FEEDBACK

Cool Down

Total Distance: Total Laps:

©poweredbychlorine.com

Dryland Training

REPS	EXERCISES	WEIGHTS/TIME	INTENSITY	NOTES/FEEDBACK

Nutrition Tracker

Breakfast	Dinner
Lunch	Snacks & Drinks

Training Schedule

TYPE	AM TIME	PM TIME	LOCATION

©poweredbychlorine.com

DAILY SWIM TRAINING LOG

Date: Location: Today's Focus:

Time: Pool: 50   25   other   Coach:

Mood: Day: M   Tu   W   Th   Fr   Sa   Su

Warm Up

REPS	DISTANCE STROKE/DRILL/KICK	INTERVAL	INTENSITY	NOTES/FEEDBACK

Pre Set

REPS	DISTANCE STROKE/DRILL/KICK	INTERVAL	INTENSITY	NOTES/FEEDBACK

Main Set

REPS	DISTANCE STROKE/DRILL/KICK	INTERVAL	INTENSITY	NOTES/FEEDBACK

Cool Down

Total Distance: Total Laps:

©poweredbychlorine.com

Dryland Training

REPS	EXERCISES	WEIGHTS/TIME	INTENSITY	NOTES/FEEDBACK

Nutrition Tracker

Breakfast	Dinner
Lunch	Snacks & Drinks

Training Schedule

TYPE	AM TIME	PM TIME	LOCATION

DAILY SWIM TRAINING LOG

Date: Location: Today's Focus:

Time: Pool: 50   25   other   Coach:

Mood: Day: M Tu W Th Fr Sa Su

Warm Up

REPS	DISTANCE STROKE/DRILL/KICK	INTERVAL	INTENSITY	NOTES/FEEDBACK

Pre Set

REPS	DISTANCE STROKE/DRILL/KICK	INTERVAL	INTENSITY	NOTES/FEEDBACK

Main Set

REPS	DISTANCE STROKE/DRILL/KICK	INTERVAL	INTENSITY	NOTES/FEEDBACK

Cool Down

Total Distance: Total Laps:

©poweredbychlorine.com

Dryland Training

REPS	EXERCISES	WEIGHTS/TIME	INTENSITY	NOTES/FEEDBACK

Nutrition Tracker

Breakfast	Dinner
Lunch	Snacks & Drinks

Training Schedule

TYPE	AM TIME	PM TIME	LOCATION

©poweredbychlorine.com

DAILY SWIM TRAINING LOG

Date:　　　　　Location:　　　　　Today's Focus:

Time:　　　　　Pool: 50　25　other　　Coach:

Mood:　　　　　　　　　　　　　　　Day: M　Tu　W　Th　Fr　Sa　Su

Warm Up

REPS	DISTANCE STROKE/DRILL/KICK	INTERVAL	INTENSITY	NOTES/FEEDBACK

Pre Set

REPS	DISTANCE STROKE/DRILL/KICK	INTERVAL	INTENSITY	NOTES/FEEDBACK

Main Set

REPS	DISTANCE STROKE/DRILL/KICK	INTERVAL	INTENSITY	NOTES/FEEDBACK

Cool Down

Total Distance:　　　　　　　　　　　Total Laps:

© poweredbychlorine.com

Dryland Training

REPS	EXERCISES	WEIGHTS/TIME	INTENSITY	NOTES/FEEDBACK

Nutrition Tracker

Breakfast	Dinner
Lunch	Snacks & Drinks

Training Schedule

TYPE	AM TIME	PM TIME	LOCATION

© poweredbychlorine.com

DAILY SWIM TRAINING LOG

Date: Location: Today's Focus:

Time: Pool: 50 25 other Coach:

Mood: Day: M Tu W Th Fr Sa Su

Warm Up

REPS	DISTANCE STROKE/DRILL/KICK	INTERVAL	INTENSITY	NOTES/FEEDBACK

Pre Set

REPS	DISTANCE STROKE/DRILL/KICK	INTERVAL	INTENSITY	NOTES/FEEDBACK

Main Set

REPS	DISTANCE STROKE/DRILL/KICK	INTERVAL	INTENSITY	NOTES/FEEDBACK

Cool Down

Total Distance: Total Laps:

Dryland Training

REPS	EXERCISES	WEIGHTS/TIME	INTENSITY	NOTES/FEEDBACK

Nutrition Tracker

Breakfast	Dinner
Lunch	Snacks & Drinks

Training Schedule

TYPE	AM TIME	PM TIME	LOCATION

ⓒpoweredbychlorine.com

DAILY SWIM TRAINING LOG

Date: Location: Today's Focus:

Time: Pool: 50   25   other   Coach:

Mood: 😀 😀 😀 😀 😀   Day: M   Tu   W   Th   Fr   Sa   Su

Warm Up

REPS	DISTANCE STROKE/DRILL/KICK	INTERVAL	INTENSITY	NOTES/FEEDBACK

Pre Set

REPS	DISTANCE STROKE/DRILL/KICK	INTERVAL	INTENSITY	NOTES/FEEDBACK

Main Set

REPS	DISTANCE STROKE/DRILL/KICK	INTERVAL	INTENSITY	NOTES/FEEDBACK

Cool Down

Total Distance: Total Laps:

© poweredbychlorine.com

Dryland Training

REPS	EXERCISES	WEIGHTS/TIME	INTENSITY	NOTES/FEEDBACK

Nutrition Tracker

Breakfast	Dinner
Lunch	Snacks & Drinks

Training Schedule

TYPE	AM TIME	PM TIME	LOCATION

©poweredbychlorine.com

DAILY SWIM TRAINING LOG

Date:　　　　　Location:　　　　　Today's Focus:

Time:　　　　　Pool: 50　25　other　　Coach:

Mood:　　　　　　　　　　　　　　Day:　M　Tu　W　Th　Fr　Sa　Su

Warm Up

REPS	DISTANCE STROKE/DRILL/KICK	INTERVAL	INTENSITY	NOTES/FEEDBACK

Pre Set

REPS	DISTANCE STROKE/DRILL/KICK	INTERVAL	INTENSITY	NOTES/FEEDBACK

Main Set

REPS	DISTANCE STROKE/DRILL/KICK	INTERVAL	INTENSITY	NOTES/FEEDBACK

Cool Down

Total Distance:　　　　　　　　　　Total Laps:

© poweredbychlorine.com

Dryland Training

REPS	EXERCISES	WEIGHTS/TIME	INTENSITY	NOTES/FEEDBACK

Nutrition Tracker

Breakfast	Dinner
Lunch	Snacks & Drinks

Training Schedule

TYPE	AM TIME	PM TIME	LOCATION

©poweredbychlorine.com

DAILY SWIM TRAINING LOG

Date: Location: Today's Focus:

Time: Pool: 50   25   other   Coach:

Mood: 😀 😊 😐 😕 😢   Day: M   Tu   W   Th   Fr   Sa   Su

Warm Up

REPS	DISTANCE STROKE/DRILL/KICK	INTERVAL	INTENSITY	NOTES/FEEDBACK

Pre Set

REPS	DISTANCE STROKE/DRILL/KICK	INTERVAL	INTENSITY	NOTES/FEEDBACK

Main Set

REPS	DISTANCE STROKE/DRILL/KICK	INTERVAL	INTENSITY	NOTES/FEEDBACK

Cool Down

Total Distance: Total Laps:

© poweredbychlorine.com

Dryland Training

REPS	EXERCISES	WEIGHTS/TIME	INTENSITY	NOTES/FEEDBACK

Nutrition Tracker

Breakfast	Dinner
Lunch	Snacks & Drinks

Training Schedule

TYPE	AM TIME	PM TIME	LOCATION

© poweredbychlorine.com

DAILY SWIM TRAINING LOG

Date:　　　　　Location:　　　　　Today's Focus:

Time:　　　　　Pool: 50　25　other　　Coach:

Mood: ⚪⚪⚪⚪⚪　　　　　　　Day:　M　Tu　W　Th　Fr　Sa　Su

Warm Up

REPS	DISTANCE STROKE/DRILL/KICK	INTERVAL	INTENSITY	NOTES/FEEDBACK

Pre Set

REPS	DISTANCE STROKE/DRILL/KICK	INTERVAL	INTENSITY	NOTES/FEEDBACK

Main Set

REPS	DISTANCE STROKE/DRILL/KICK	INTERVAL	INTENSITY	NOTES/FEEDBACK

Cool Down

Total Distance:　　　　　　　　　　　Total Laps:

©poweredbychlorine.com

Dryland Training

REPS	EXERCISES	WEIGHTS/TIME	INTENSITY	NOTES/FEEDBACK

Nutrition Tracker

Breakfast	Dinner
Lunch	Snacks & Drinks

Training Schedule

TYPE	AM TIME	PM TIME	LOCATION

DAILY SWIM TRAINING LOG

Date: Location: Today's Focus:

Time: Pool: 50   25   other   Coach:

Mood: Day: M   Tu   W   Th   Fr   Sa   Su

Warm Up

REPS	DISTANCE STROKE/DRILL/KICK	INTERVAL	INTENSITY	NOTES/FEEDBACK

Pre Set

REPS	DISTANCE STROKE/DRILL/KICK	INTERVAL	INTENSITY	NOTES/FEEDBACK

Main Set

REPS	DISTANCE STROKE/DRILL/KICK	INTERVAL	INTENSITY	NOTES/FEEDBACK

Cool Down

Total Distance: Total Laps:

© poweredbychlorine.com

Dryland Training

REPS	EXERCISES	WEIGHTS/TIME	INTENSITY	NOTES/FEEDBACK

Nutrition Tracker

Breakfast	Dinner
Lunch	Snacks & Drinks

Training Schedule

TYPE	AM TIME	PM TIME	LOCATION

© poweredbychlorine.com

DAILY SWIM TRAINING LOG

Date: Location: Today's Focus:

Time: Pool: 50   25   other   Coach:

Mood: Day: M Tu W Th Fr Sa Su

Warm Up

REPS	DISTANCE STROKE/DRILL/KICK	INTERVAL	INTENSITY	NOTES/FEEDBACK

Pre Set

REPS	DISTANCE STROKE/DRILL/KICK	INTERVAL	INTENSITY	NOTES/FEEDBACK

Main Set

REPS	DISTANCE STROKE/DRILL/KICK	INTERVAL	INTENSITY	NOTES/FEEDBACK

Cool Down

Total Distance: Total Laps:

©poweredbychlorine.com

Dryland Training

REPS	EXERCISES	WEIGHTS/TIME	INTENSITY	NOTES/FEEDBACK

Nutrition Tracker

Breakfast	Dinner
Lunch	Snacks & Drinks

Training Schedule

TYPE	AM TIME	PM TIME	LOCATION

© poweredbychlorine.com

DAILY SWIM TRAINING LOG

Date: Location: Today's Focus:

Time: Pool: 50   25   other   Coach:

Mood: Day: M   Tu   W   Th   Fr   Sa   Su

Warm Up

REPS	DISTANCE STROKE/DRILL/KICK	INTERVAL	INTENSITY	NOTES/FEEDBACK

Pre Set

REPS	DISTANCE STROKE/DRILL/KICK	INTERVAL	INTENSITY	NOTES/FEEDBACK

Main Set

REPS	DISTANCE STROKE/DRILL/KICK	INTERVAL	INTENSITY	NOTES/FEEDBACK

Cool Down

Total Distance: Total Laps:

©poweredbychlorine.com

Dryland Training

REPS	EXERCISES	WEIGHTS/TIME	INTENSITY	NOTES/FEEDBACK

Nutrition Tracker

Breakfast	Dinner
Lunch	Snacks & Drinks

Training Schedule

TYPE	AM TIME	PM TIME	LOCATION

©poweredbychlorine.com

DAILY SWIM TRAINING LOG

Date: Location: Today's Focus:

Time: Pool: 50   25   other   Coach:

Mood: Day: M Tu W Th Fr Sa Su

Warm Up

REPS	DISTANCE STROKE/DRILL/KICK	INTERVAL	INTENSITY	NOTES/FEEDBACK

Pre Set

REPS	DISTANCE STROKE/DRILL/KICK	INTERVAL	INTENSITY	NOTES/FEEDBACK

Main Set

REPS	DISTANCE STROKE/DRILL/KICK	INTERVAL	INTENSITY	NOTES/FEEDBACK

Cool Down

Total Distance: Total Laps:

© poweredbychlorine.com

Dryland Training

REPS	EXERCISES	WEIGHTS/TIME	INTENSITY	NOTES/FEEDBACK

Nutrition Tracker

Breakfast	Dinner
Lunch	Snacks & Drinks

Training Schedule

TYPE	AM TIME	PM TIME	LOCATION

©poweredbychlorine.com

DAILY SWIM TRAINING LOG

Date: Location: Today's Focus:

Time: Pool: 50   25   other   Coach:

Mood: Day: M   Tu   W   Th   Fr   Sa   Su

Warm Up

REPS	DISTANCE STROKE/DRILL/KICK	INTERVAL	INTENSITY	NOTES/FEEDBACK

Pre Set

REPS	DISTANCE STROKE/DRILL/KICK	INTERVAL	INTENSITY	NOTES/FEEDBACK

Main Set

REPS	DISTANCE STROKE/DRILL/KICK	INTERVAL	INTENSITY	NOTES/FEEDBACK

Cool Down

Total Distance: Total Laps:

© poweredbychlorine.com

Dryland Training

REPS	EXERCISES	WEIGHTS/TIME	INTENSITY	NOTES/FEEDBACK

Nutrition Tracker

Breakfast	Dinner
Lunch	Snacks & Drinks

Training Schedule

TYPE	AM TIME	PM TIME	LOCATION

DAILY SWIM TRAINING LOG

Date: Location: Today's Focus:

Time: Pool: 50   25   other   Coach:

Mood: 😀 😀 😀 😀   Day: M   Tu   W   Th   Fr   Sa   Su

Warm Up

REPS	DISTANCE STROKE/DRILL/KICK	INTERVAL	INTENSITY	NOTES/FEEDBACK

Pre Set

REPS	DISTANCE STROKE/DRILL/KICK	INTERVAL	INTENSITY	NOTES/FEEDBACK

Main Set

REPS	DISTANCE STROKE/DRILL/KICK	INTERVAL	INTENSITY	NOTES/FEEDBACK

Cool Down

Total Distance: Total Laps:

©poweredbychlorine.com

Dryland Training

REPS	EXERCISES	WEIGHTS/TIME	INTENSITY	NOTES/FEEDBACK

Nutrition Tracker

Breakfast	Dinner
Lunch	Snacks & Drinks

Training Schedule

TYPE	AM TIME	PM TIME	LOCATION

©poweredbychlorine.com

DAILY SWIM TRAINING LOG

Date:	Location:	Today's Focus:

Time:	Pool: 50 25 other	Coach:

Mood:	Day: M Tu W Th Fr Sa Su

Warm Up

REPS	DISTANCE STROKE/DRILL/KICK	INTERVAL	INTENSITY	NOTES/FEEDBACK

Pre Set

REPS	DISTANCE STROKE/DRILL/KICK	INTERVAL	INTENSITY	NOTES/FEEDBACK

Main Set

REPS	DISTANCE STROKE/DRILL/KICK	INTERVAL	INTENSITY	NOTES/FEEDBACK

Cool Down

Total Distance:	Total Laps:

©poweredbychlorine.com

Dryland Training

REPS	EXERCISES	WEIGHTS/TIME	INTENSITY	NOTES/FEEDBACK

Nutrition Tracker

Breakfast	Dinner
Lunch	Snacks & Drinks

Training Schedule

TYPE	AM TIME	PM TIME	LOCATION

PB TRACKER

Date	Pool Type	Location	Stroke	Distance	PB Time	External Factors	Internal Factors

© poweredbychlorine.com

PB TRACKER

Date	Pool Type	Location	Stroke	Distance	PB Time	External Factors	Internal Factors

©poweredbychlorine.com

PB TRACKER

Date	Pool Type	Location	Stroke	Distance	PB Time	External Factors	Internal Factors

©poweredbychlorine.com